Three Occasional Pieces

Other works by Samuel Beckett

published by Faber and Faber

ALL THAT FALL: A Play for Radio
ENDGAME: A Play in One Act *and* ACT WITHOUT WORDS
ENDS AND ODDS: Plays and Sketches
FOOTFALLS
HAPPY DAYS: A Play in Two Acts
KRAPP'S LAST TAPE *and* EMBERS
NOT I
WAITING FOR GODOT: A Tragicomedy in Two Acts

published by Calder and Boyars

COLLECTED POEMS IN ENGLISH AND FRENCH
COME AND GO
COMPANY
FIRST LOVE
FOR TO END YET AGAIN *and* OTHER FIZZLES
FOUR NOVELLAS
HOW IT IS
IMAGINATION DEAD IMAGINE
MALONE DIES
MERCIER AND CAMIER
MOLLOY
MORE PRICKS THAN KICKS
MURPHY
NO'S KNIFE
POEMS IN ENGLISH
PROUST *and*
THREE DIALOGUES WITH GEORGES DUTHUIT
SIX RESIDUA
STILLS
TEXTS FOR NOTHING
THE UNNAMABLE
WATT

Three Occasional Pieces

by

SAMUEL BECKETT

faber and faber

First published in 1982
by Faber and Faber Limited
3 Queen Square London WC1N 3AU
Printed in Great Britain by
Latimer Trend & Company Ltd Plymouth
All rights reserved

Applications for the performing rights of
the dramatic works included in this volume
should be addressed to
Spokesmen, 1 Craven Hill, London W2

British Library Cataloguing in Publication Data

Beckett, Samuel
Three occasional pieces.
I. Title
822'.912   PR6003.E282
ISBN 0-571-11800-3

CONTENTS

A Piece of Monologue, written for David Warrilow, was performed by him in 1980 in New York and elsewhere in the United States, directed by David Warrilow and Rocky Greenberg.

Rockaby was written for a seminar in Buffalo in 1981. Its first production there was played by Billie Whitelaw and directed by Alan Schneider.

Ohio Impromptu was written for a seminar at Ohio State University in 1981. Its first production was played by David Warrilow (the reader) and Rand Mitchell (the listener) and directed by Alan Schneider.

A Piece of Monologue

Curtain.
Faint diffuse light.
Speaker stands well off centre downstage audience left.
White hair, white nightgown, white socks.
Two metres to his left, same level, same height, standard lamp, skull-sized white globe, faintly lit.
Just visible extreme right, same level, white foot of pallet bed.
Ten seconds before speech begins.
Thirty seconds before end of speech lamplight begins to fail.
Lamp out. Silence. SPEAKER, *globe, foot of pallet, barely visible in diffuse light.*
Ten seconds.
Curtain.

SPEAKER: Birth was the death of him. Again. Words are few. Dying too. Birth was the death of him. Ghastly grinning ever since. Up at the lid to come. In cradle and crib. At suck first fiasco. With the first totters. From mammy to nanny and back. All the way. Bandied back and forth. So ghastly grinning on. From funeral to funeral. To now. This night. Two and a half billion seconds. Again. Two and a half billion seconds. Hard to believe so few. From funeral to funeral. Funerals of . . . he all but said of loved ones. Thirty thousand nights. Hard to believe so few. Born dead of night. Sun long sunk behind the larches. New needles turning green. In the room dark gaining. Till faint light from standard lamp. Wick turned low. And now. This night. Up at nightfall. Every nightfall. Faint light in room. Whence unknown. None from window. No. Next to none. No such thing as none. Gropes to window and stares out. Stands there staring out. Stock still staring out. Nothing stirring in that black vast. Gropes back in the end to where the lamp is standing. Was standing. When last went out. Loose matches in right-hand pocket. Strikes one on his buttock the way his father taught him. Takes off milk white globe and sets it down. Match goes out. Strikes a second as before. Takes off chimney. Smoke-clouded. Holds it in left hand. Match goes out. Strikes a third as before and sets it to wick. Puts back chimney. Match goes out. Puts back globe. Turns wick low. Backs away to edge of light and turns to face east. Blank wall. So nightly. Up. Socks. Nightgown. Window. Lamp. Backs away to edge of light and stands facing blank wall. Covered with pictures once. Pictures of . . . he all but said of loved ones. Unframed. Unglazed. Pinned to wall with drawing-pins. All shapes and sizes. Down one after another. Gone. Torn to shreds and scattered. Strewn all over the floor. Not at one sweep. No sudden fit of . . . no word. Ripped from the wall and torn to shreds one by one. Over the years. Years of nights. Nothing on the wall now but the pins. Not all. Some out with the wrench. Some still pinning a shred. So stands there facing blank wall.

Dying on. No more no less. No. Less. Less to die. Ever less. Like light at nightfall. Stands there facing east. Blank pinpocked surface once white in shadow. Could once name them all. There was father. That grey void. There mother. That other. There together. Smiling. Wedding day. There all three. That grey blot. There alone. He alone. So on. Not now. Forgotten. All gone so long. Gone. Ripped off and torn to shreds. Scattered all over the floor. Swept out of the way under the bed and left. Thousand shreds under the bed with the dust and spiders. All the . . . he all but said the loved ones. Stands there facing the wall staring beyond. Nothing there either. Nothing stirring there either. Nothing stirring anywhere. Nothing to be seen anywhere. Nothing to be heard anywhere. Room once full of sounds. Faint sounds. Whence unknown. Fewer and fainter as time wore on.

Nights wore on. None now. No. No such thing as none.
Rain some nights still slant against the panes. Or dropping
gentle on the place beneath. Even now. Lamp smoking
though wick turned low. Strange. Faint smoke issuing
through vent in globe. Low ceiling stained by night after
night of this. Dark shapeless blot on surface elsewhere white.
Once white. Stands facing wall after the various motions
described. That is up at nightfall and into gown and socks.
No. In them already. In them all night. All day. All day
and night. Up at nightfall in gown and socks and after a
moment to get his bearings gropes to window. Faint light in
room. Unutterably faint. Whence unknown. Stands stock
still staring out. Into black vast. Nothing there. Nothing
stirring. That he can see. Hear. Dwells thus as if unable to
move again. Or no will left to move again. Not enough will
left to move again. Turns in the end and gropes to where he
knows the lamp is standing. Thinks he knows. Was last
standing. When last went out. Match one as described for
globe. Two for chimney. Three for wick. Chimney and
globe back on. Turns wick low. Backs away to edge of light
and turns to face wall. East. Still as the lamp by his side.
Gown and socks white to take faint light. Once white. Hair
white to take faint light. Foot of pallet just visible edge of
frame. Once white to take faint light. Stands there staring
beyond. Nothing. Empty dark. Till first word always the
same. Night after night the same. Birth. Then slow fade up
of a faint form. Out of the dark. A window. Looking west.
Sun long sunk behind the larches. Light dying. Soon none
left to die. No. No such thing as no light. Starless moonless
heaven. Dies on to dawn and never dies. There in the dark
that window. Night slowly falling. Eyes to the small pane
gaze at that first night. Turn from it in the end to face the
darkened room. There in the end slowly a faint hand.
Holding aloft a lighted spill. In light of spill faintly the hand
and milkwhite globe. Then second hand. In light of spill.
Takes off globe and disappears. Reappears empty. Takes off
chimney. Two hands and chimney in light of spill. Spill to
wick. Chimney back on. Hand with spill disappears. Second

hand disappears. Chimney alone in gloom. Hand reappears
with globe. Globe back on. Turns wick low. Disappears. Pale
globe alone in gloom. Glimmer of brass bedrail. Fade. Birth
the death of him. That nevoid smile. Thirty thousand nights.
Stands at edge of lamplight staring beyond. Into dark whole
again. Window gone. Hands gone. Light gone. Gone. Again
and again. Again and again gone. Till dark slowly parts
again. Grey light. Rain pelting. Umbrellas round a grave.
Seen from above. Streaming black canopies. Black ditch
beneath. Rain bubbling in the black mud. Empty for the
moment. That place beneath. Which . . . he all but said
which loved one? Thirty seconds. To add to the two and a
half billion odd. Then fade. Dark whole again. Blest dark.
No. No such thing as whole. Stands staring beyond half
hearing what he's saying. He? The words falling from his
mouth. Making do with his mouth. Lights lamp as described.
Backs away to edge of light and turns to face wall. Stares
beyond into dark. Waits for first word always the same. It
gathers in his mouth. Parts lips and thrusts tongue forward.
Birth. Parts the dark. Slowly the window. That first night.
The room. The spill. The hands. The lamp. The gleam of
brass. Fade. Gone. Again and again. Again and again gone.
Mouth agape. A cry. Stifled by nasal. Dark parts. Grey light.
Rain pelting. Streaming umbrellas. Ditch. Bubbling black
mud. Coffin out of frame. Whose? Fade. Gone. Move on to
other matters. Try to move on. To other matters. How far
from wall? Head almost touching. As at window. Eyes glued
to pane staring out. Nothing stirring. Black vast. Stands there
stock still staring out as if unable to move again. Or gone the
will to move again. Gone. Faint cry in his ear. Mouth agape.
Closed with hiss of breath. Lips joined. Feel soft touch of
lip on lip. Lip lipping lip. Then parted by cry as before.
Where is he now? Back at window staring out. Eyes glued
to pane. As if looking his last. Turns away at last and gropes
through faint unaccountable light to unseen lamp. White
gown moving through that gloom. Once white. Lights and
moves to face wall as described. Head almost touching.
Stands there staring beyond waiting for first word. It

gathers in his mouth. Birth. Parts lips and thrusts tongue
between them. Tip of tongue. Feel soft touch of tongue on
lips. Of lips on tongue. Fade up in outer dark of window.
Stare beyond through rift in dark to other dark. Further
dark. Sun long sunk behind the larches. Nothing stirring.
Nothing faintly stirring. Stock still eyes glued to pane. As if
looking his last. At that first night. Of thirty thousand odd.
Turn away in the end to darkened room. Where soon to be.
This night to be. Spill. Hands. Lamp. Gleam of brass. Pale
globe alone in gloom. Brass bedrail catching light. Thirty
seconds. To swell the two and a half billion odd. Fade.
Gone. Cry. Snuffed with breath of nostrils. Again and again.
Again and again gone. Till whose grave? Which . . . he all
but said which loved one's? He? Black ditch in pelting rain.
Way out through the grey rift in dark. Seen from on high.
Streaming canopies. Bubbling black mud. Coffin on its way.
Loved one . . . he all but said loved one on his way. Her
way. Thirty seconds. Fade. Gone. Stands there staring
beyond. Into dark whole again. No. No such thing as whole.
Head almost touching wall. White hair catching light. White
gown. White socks. White foot of pallet edge of frame stage
left. Once white. Least . . . give and head rests on wall.
But no. Stock still head haught staring beyond. Nothing
stirring. Faintly stirring. Thirty thousand nights of ghosts
beyond. Beyond that black beyond. Ghost light. Ghost
nights. Ghost rooms. Ghost graves. Ghost . . . he all but
said ghost loved ones. Waiting on the rip word. Stands there
staring beyond at that black veil lips quivering to half-heard
words. Treating of other matters. Trying to treat of other
matters. Till half hears there are no other matters. Never
were other matters. Never two matters. Never but the one
matter. The dead and gone. The dying and the going. From
the word go. The word begone. Such as the light going
now. Beginning to go. In the room. Where else? Unnoticed
by him staring beyond. The globe alone. Not the other.
The unaccountable. From nowhere. On all sides nowhere.
Unutterably faint. The globe alone. Alone gone.

15

Rockaby

NOTES

Light:
Subdued on chair. Rest of stage dark.
Subdued spot on face constant throughout, unaffected by successive fades. Either wide enough to include narrow limits of rock or concentrated on face when still or at mid-rock. Then throughout speech face slightly swaying in and out of light.
Opening fade-up: first spot on face alone, long pause, then light on chair.
Final fade-out: first chair, long pause with spot on face alone, head slowly sinks, come to rest, fade out spot.

W:
Prematurely old. Unkempt grey hair. Huge eyes in white expressionless face. White hands holding ends of armrests.

Eyes:
Now closed, now open in unblinking gaze. About equal proportions section 1, increasingly closed 2 and 3, closed for good halfway through 4.

Costume:
Black lacy high-necked evening gown. Long sleeves. Jet sequins to glitter when rocking. Incongruous flimsy head-dress set askew with extravagant trimming to catch light when rocking.

Attitude:
Completely still till fade-out of chair. Then in light of spot head slowly inclined.

Chair:
Pale wood highly polished to gleam when rocking. Footrest. Vertical back. Rounded inward curving arms to suggest embrace.

Rock:
Slight. Slow. Controlled mechanically without assistance from W.

Voice:
Towards end of 4, say from 'saying to herself' on, gradually softer. Lines in italics spoken by W with V. A little softer each time. W's 'more' a little softer each time.

W: *Woman in chair.*
V: *Her recorded voice.*
Fade up on W in rocking-chair facing front downstage slightly off centre audience left.
Long pause.

W: More.
  (*Pause. Rock and voice together.*)
V: till in the end
   the day came
   in the end came
   close of a long day
   when she said
   to herself
   whom else
   time she stopped
   time she stopped
   going to and fro
   all eyes
   all sides
   high and low
   for another
   another like herself
   another creature like herself
   a little like
   going to and fro
   all eyes
   all sides

high and low
for another
till in the end
close of a long day
to herself
whom else
time she stopped
time she stopped
going to and fro
all eyes
all sides
high and low
for another
another living soul
going to and fro
all eyes like herself
all sides
high and low
for another
another like herself
a little like
going to and fro
till in the end
close of a long day
to herself
whom else
time she stopped
going to and fro
time she stopped
time she stopped
(*Together: echo of 'time she stopped', coming to rest of rock,
faint fade of light.
Long pause.*)
W: More.
(*Pause. Rock and voice together.*)
V: so in the end
close of a long day
went back in

in the end went back in
saying to herself
whom else
time she stopped
time she stopped
going to and fro
time she went and sat
at her window
quiet at her window
facing other windows
so in the end
close of a long day
in the end went and sat
went back in and sat
at her window
let up the blind and sat
quiet at her window
only window
facing other windows
other only windows
all eyes
all sides
high and low
for another
at her window
another like herself
a little like
another living soul
one other living soul
at her window
gone in like herself
gone back in
in the end
close of a long day
saying to herself
whom else
time she stopped
time she stopped

going to and fro
time she went and sat
at her window
quiet at her window
only window
facing other windows
other only windows
all eyes
all sides
high and low
for another
another like herself
a little like
another living soul
one other living soul
    (*Together: echo of 'living soul', coming to rest of rock, faint*
    fade of light.
    Long pause.)
W: More.
    (*Pause. Rock and voice together.*)
V: till in the end
the day came
in the end came
close of a long day
sitting at her window
quiet at her window
only window
facing other windows
other only windows
all blinds down
never one up
hers alone up
till the day came
in the end came
close of a long day
sitting at her window
quiet at her window
all eyes

22

all sides
high and low
for a blind up
one blind up
no more
never mind a face
behind the pane
famished eyes
like hers
to see
be seen
no
a blind up
like hers
a little like
one blind up no more
another creature there
somewhere there
behind the pane
another living soul
one other living soul
till the day came
in the end came
close of a long day
when she said
to herself
whom else
time she stopped
time she stopped
sitting at her window
quiet at her window
only window
facing other windows
other only windows
all eyes
all sides
high and low
time she stopped

time she stopped
   (*Together: echo of 'time she stopped', coming to rest of rock,*
   faint fade of light.
   Long pause.)
W: More.
   (*Pause. Rock and voice together.*)
V: so in the end
   close of a long day
   went down
   in the end went down
   down the steep stair
   let down the blind and down
   right down
   into the old rocker
   mother rocker
   where mother rocked
   all the years
   all in black
   best black
   sat and rocked
   rocked
   till her end came
   in the end came
   off her head they said
   gone off her head
   but harmless
   no harm in her
   dead one day
   no
   night
   dead one night
   in the rocker
   in her best black
   head fallen
   and the rocker rocking
   rocking away
   so in the end
   close of a long day

went down
in the end went down
down the steep stair
let down the blind and down
right down
into the old rocker
those arms at last
and rocked
rocked
with closed eyes
closing eyes
she so long all eyes
famished eyes
all sides
high and low
to and fro
at her window
to see
be seen
till in the end
close of a long day
to herself
whom else
time she stopped
let down the blind and stopped
time she went down
down the steep stair
time she went right down
was her own other
own other living soul
so in the end
close of a long day
went down
let down the blind and down
right down
into the old rocker
and rocked
rocked

saying to herself
no
done with that
the rocker
those arms at last
saying to the rocker
rock her off
stop her eyes
fuck life
stop her eyes
rock her off
rock her off
 (*Together: echo of 'rock her off', coming to rest of rock, slow
 fade out.*)

Ohio Impromptu

L = Listener.
R = Reader.
As alike in appearance as possible.
Light on table midstage. Rest of stage in darkness.
Plain white deal table say 8′ × 4′.
Two plain armless white deal chairs.
L seated at table facing front towards end of long side audience right.
Bowed head propped on right hand. Face hidden. Left hand on table.
Long black coat. Long white hair.
R seated at table in profile centre of short side audience right. Bowed
head propped on right hand. Left hand on table. Book on table before
him open at last pages. Long black coat. Long white hair.
Black wide-brimmed hat at centre of table.
Fade up.
Ten seconds
R turns page.
Pause.

R: (*Reading*) Little is left to tell. In a last—
   (*L knocks with left hand on table.*)
   Little is left to tell.
   (*Pause. Knock*)
   In a last attempt to obtain relief he moved from where they
   had been so long together to a single room on the far bank.
   From its single window he could see the downstream
   extremity of the Isle of Swans.
   (*Pause*)
   Relief he had hoped would flow from unfamiliarity.

29

Unfamiliar room. Unfamiliar scene. Out to where nothing
ever shared. Back to where nothing ever shared. From this
he had once half hoped some measure of relief might flow.
(*Pause*)
Day after day he could be seen slowly pacing the islet. Hour
after hour. In his long black coat no matter what the weather
and old world Latin Quarter hat. At the tip he would always
pause to dwell on the receding stream. How in joyous eddies
its two arms conflowed and flowed united on. Then turn and
his slow steps retrace.
(*Pause*)
In his dreams—
(*Knock*)
Then turn and his slow steps retrace.
(*Pause. Knock*)
In his dreams he had been warned against this change. Seen
the dear face and heard the unspoken words, Stay where we
were so long alone together, my shade will comfort you.
(*Pause*)
Could he not—
(*Knock*)
Seen the dear face and heard the unspoken words, Stay
where we were so long alone together, my shade will comfort
you.
(*Pause. Knock*)
Could he not now turn back? Acknowledge his error and
return to where they were once so long alone together.
Alone together so much shared. No. What he had done alone
could not be undone. Nothing he had ever done alone
could ever be undone. By him alone.
(*Pause*)
In this extremity his old terror of night laid hold on him
again. After so long a lapse that as if never been. (*Pause.
Looks closer.*) Yes, after so long a lapse that as if never been.
Now with redoubled force the fearful symptoms described at
length page forty paragraph four. (*Starts to turn back the
pages. Checked by L's left hand. Resumes relinquished page.*)
White nights now again his portion. As when his heart was

30

young. No sleep no braving sleep till—(*Turns page.*)—dawn of day.
(*Pause*)
Little is left to tell. One night—
(*Knock*)
Little is left to tell.
(*Pause. Knock*)
One night as he sat trembling head in hands from head to foot a man appeared to him and said, I have been sent by— and here he named the dear name—to comfort you. Then drawing a worn volume from the pocket of his long black coat he sat and read till dawn. Then disappeared without a word.
(*Pause*)
Some time later he appeared again at the same hour with the same volume and this time without preamble sat and read it through again the long night through. Then disappeared without a word.
(*Pause*)
So from time to time unheralded he would appear to read the sad tale through again and the long night away. Then disappear without a word.
(*Pause*)
With never a word exchanged they grew to be as one.
(*Pause*)
Till the night came at last when having closed the book and dawn at hand he did not disappear but sat on without a word.
(*Pause*)
Finally he said, I have had word from—and here he named the dear name—that I shall not come again. I saw the dear face and heard the unspoken words, No need to go to him again, even were it in your power.
(*Pause*)
So the sad—
(*Knock*)
Saw the dear face and heard the unspoken words, No need to go to him again, even were it in your power.

31

(*Pause. Knock*)
So the sad tale a last time told they sat on as though turned
to stone. Through the single window dawn shed no light.
From the street no sound of reawakening. Or was it that
buried in who knows what thoughts they paid no heed? To
light of day. To sound of reawakening. What thoughts who
knows. Thoughts, no, not thoughts. Profounds of mind.
Buried in who knows what profounds of mind. Of
mindlessness. Whither no light can reach. No sound. So sat
on as though turned to stone. The sad tale a last time told.
(*Pause*)
Nothing is left to tell.
(*Pause. R makes to close book.*
Knock. Book half closed.)
Nothing is left to tell.
(*Pause. R closes book.*
Knock.
Silence. Five seconds.
Simultaneously they lower their right hands to table, raise their
heads and look at each other. Unblinking. Expressionless.
Ten seconds.
Fade out.)